DOWN THE DEEP LANES

DEVON
BOOKS

FOR
OLIVE COOK
AND
EDWIN SMITH

DOWN THE DEEP LANES

PETER BEACHAM

Photographs
JAMES RAVILIOUS

foreword by
CANDIDA LYCETT-GREEN

Published in 2000 by Devon Books
Reprinted in 2001

ISBN
1 85522 743 6

DEVON BOOKS
Official Publisher to Devon County Council
Halsgrove House
Lower Moor Way
Tiverton Devon EX16 6SS
Tel: 01884 243242
Fax: 01884 243325
www.halsgrove.com

Devon Books acknowledges the support of the Countryside Agency,
North Devon District Council and Torridge District Council for
this publication, which promotes the aims of the
Northern Devon Local Cultural Strategy.

Title Page
View towards Dartmoor near Winkleigh

Designed by Toby Matthews
Typeset by The Bardwell Press, Oxford
Printed by Bolis Poligrafiche, Italy

Contents

Above
Jo Curzon and her flock, Dolton

Acknowledgements

We must first acknowledge our indebtedness to the people of Devon and beyond for their unfailing courtesy in allowing us to make themselves, their homes, working lives, landscapes, and places of worship the subject matter of this book. Of the many pleasures we have had in its making, the warmth of their welcome and their interest in our project will always remain memorable. They sustain this beloved landscape, often against seemingly insuperable odds, and we hope we pay some small tribute to them in these pages.

We owe much to those many influences on our lives that have shaped our understanding of what we are looking at. Some of these have been explored in Peter Hamilton's recent book on James Ravilious's work, *An English Eye*, and other important published points of reference for both of us are included in the bibliography. Our dedication of this book to Olive Cook and Edwin Smith records our admiration for their lifetime achievement in publishing words and photographs that are mutually instructive and wonderfully complement each other.

The majority of James's photographs come from his work for the Beaford Archive and we fully acknowledge the Beaford Centre, his base for so many years. Some of the orchard photographs were commissioned by the environmental charity, Common Ground, whose influence pervades this book.

Then there are the more personal thanks. For me the poetry of Ted Hughes has been a special source of inspiration: indeed our title is the last line of *Last Load*, from his *Moortown* collection written out of his experience of farming in west Devon. We are very grateful to Carol Hughes, and to Faber and Faber Ltd. for gratis permission to quote from his work, and also some lines from T S Eliot and Philip Larkin. Paul Dadson kindly allowed me to read his unpublished thesis on corrugated iron and Roger Thorne first aroused my interest in chapels many years ago. My father Ian Beacham and my wife Chrissie read some of the early versions of the text and made many helpful suggestions. Diana Marriott and Robin Ravilious read the whole text meticulously: it has been much improved by their thoughtful contributions and sustained interest. And our families have supported our preoccupations, endless discussions and expeditions with their well-practised patience and goodwill.

We would like to thank Peter Hamilton and Toby Matthews of the Bardwell Press for putting the book together, and Alan Winn for printing the photographs with great skill and dedication. They have been a joy to work with.

Finally, I am allowed the author's privilege of acknowledging my debt to James Ravilious. The idea for the present work sprang out of our collaboration on another book some years ago, but I was not to know that working together on this one would be such a great and enduring pleasure.

PETER BEACHAM
Exeter
Easter 1999

Above
Pig at the edge of the wood, Millhams, Dolton

Foreword

by Candida Lycett-Green

Like the Ted Hughes poem the line comes from, *Down the Deep Lanes* is a revelation. It is not the stuff of ordinary guide books eulogising the familiar front of Devon — the legendary looks of Widecombe in the Moor, the sensational sea front at Sidmouth; instead, it is a beautifully painted portrait of the back. It shows us the ordinary, unsung, everyday side of the county which we all take for granted — the cattle ambling home for milking along fern-banked lanes, the ramshackle barns, the cob buildings and corrugated iron sheds which have grown out of their surroundings and evolved over time and through necessity, the Methodist chapels and old orchards, the village men, young and old, ringing out the bells in some belfry high over the churchyard.

Above all this book is about the continuance of things. Many of the marvellous and inspiring photographs by James Ravilious have been taken in the last three years yet they depict a story and tell of traditions which are centuries old. The terrain of Devon dictates the way men fashion it. Its ten thousand miles of lanes cannot easily be tidied up with kerbstones and widened to suit Euro lorries, for their paths are too sinuous and the hills over which they snake too steep.

Devon will always keep its strong and inimitable character, one which Peter Beacham knows so well for he has spent so much of his life travelling its deep lanes: there cannot be a village or hamlet he has not visited nor a church door he has not opened. His work has led him down myriad rutted, muddy tracks to forgotten ancient farms and up steep attic stairs into the roofs of mouldering manor houses. His love of Devon is profound, his descriptions heartfelt and lyrical — but never sentimental. His Devon moves majestically into the next millennium with a tide of late twentieth century clutter — power lines and mobile phone masts included — in its wake. Throughout this book there are echoes of Eliot's description in *East Coker*:

> … Now the light falls
> Across the green field, leaving the deep lane
> Shuttered with branches, dark in the afternoon,
> Where you lean against a bank while a van passes,
> And the deep lane insists on the direction
> Into the village, in the electric heat
> Hypnotised …

Above
St Nonna church and gatehouse, Bradstone

Overleaf
Farrier, Bradstone

Introduction

The best guide books fire their readers with enthusiasm to go off and discover somewhere for themselves, allowing the imagination to roam freely and make the journey in the mind's eye before making it on the ground. Part descriptive, part interpretive, such books persuade us there is much more to be enjoyed than can possibly be conveyed in words and pictures. The literature of Devon frequently employs words like 'remote' 'hidden' 'secret' and 'little-known' to describe the sequestered countryside that has always characterised this county and that still survives miraculously intact in many parts today, especially down the lane to the farm: words that combine a sense of endless exploration and of discoveries still to be made with an underlying assurance that the mystery of this landscape will never be fully revealed.

This book takes the reader on a journey down Devon's deep lanes. What we see might seem minor, obvious or even eccentric, but it is the stuff of every-day existence which is more important than the great panoramas, famous country houses and much visited show villages in defining the character of the countryside and contributing to a sense of regional identity. So we have chosen corrugated iron, the farmstead and the chapel rather than thatch, the village and the parish church, topics that are often generously treated in the guide books. Some of our subjects – such as cob, the vegetable garden and the orchard – are overlooked for their ordinariness or, like churchyards and country lanes, simply taken for granted. Others – especially the belfry and the quarry – have to be sought out because they are set apart and, for different reasons, sometimes misunderstood or even resented. And throughout these pages there is much more about mud and manure than sun and sand.

In an obvious sense the book has a particular geography because it is inspired by the landscape of Devon, especially the country between the rivers Taw and Torridge, but we have extended westward into Cornwall and eastward

Above
Woodpile near Iddesleigh

into Somerset where the themes flow naturally across county boundaries. And in another, perhaps more important way, it is not limited to a particular part of England: it is about such little known, unregarded and uncelebrated aspects of ordinary life and landscape anywhere. Ordinary lives are actually extraordinary, often heroic and humorous in equal part; the commonplace turns out to have uniqueness, the familiar is too rarely savoured for the richness and diversity there is on offer every day.

We have both had the immense good fortune to spend almost the whole of our working lives in the countryside of Devon, day by day moving around in its landscape, seeing its buildings, meeting its people. Since this period has spanned the last three decades of the twentieth century we have, of course, seen huge changes in rural life but we can also happily report on the underlying strength and continuity of tradition. What you will find here is at one level simply a record of our experience. But because it is also a portrait of the contemporary countryside, it is a gentle plea for the recognition of those indefinable qualities that contribute to the spirit of the place and that can never be artificially created. All the subjects we describe and illustrate here deserve to be better appreciated, understood, loved. It would please us if the day dawns when corrugated iron is as sought after as thatch, protesters march to demand the reopening of the local quarry, and guide books tell us how often it rains.

Above
Ivor Brock walking up West Lane, Dolton

Lane

What visitors often remember most vividly about Devon is being denied the view. Having been offered the prospect of some of the richest landscape in England, they find themselves travelling mile after mile along lanes sunk in deep hollows between huge earth banks and thick hedges: even the natives' sense of direction sometimes wavers on such expeditions. But when the rare vantage point is finally discovered, it will have been well worth the wait. Though more usually glimpse than panorama, the patchwork of fields, woods and farms threaded together by its lanes immediately engages the imagination. The eye may be drawn to trace the secret route of a single lane, at first seeming to ramble to nowhere in particular, only faintly discernible in the thickness of a double hedge, occasionally confirmed by a brief shining of tarmac in the middle distance. And then, as it disappears over the horizon, the mind's eye can begin to roam freely over the mystery of this hidden, secluded country.

Such exploration plunges the traveller deep into the making of the English landscape. These common roads represent an ancient pattern of communication that has evolved over more than 5000 years. What today is a narrow country lane of little importance may have been the principal route between major medieval towns five or six centuries ago: when seen in this light, the curiously over-large medieval churches in settlements along its length, long since by-passed by more modern roads, will suddenly make sense. Almost anywhere in England a journey of a few miles will be defined by such references to the long history of the countryside: prehistoric earthworks, Anglo-Saxon estate boundaries, medieval field patterns, eighteenth-century emparkment and perhaps some nineteenth-century enclosure. It will all still be there, only needing to be recognised in the steepness of a hedge bank, the shape of a field or a sudden bend in the lane.

Below
Horace Baker laying a hedge, Dolton

Right
Road gang near Iddesleigh

Overleaf
Towards Iddesleigh and Dartmoor

And all this time the network of lanes has served as the matrix of rural life. At the primary level they are the highways of the farm along which stock and machinery have always been moved between fields and holdings. They are also the link with the wider world, represented by the school bus, milk tanker, cattle-truck, mini-bus, post-van and all those unsung services that hold the community together. The summer visitor may delight in grass greening the middle of the lane and verges so high the car can hardly pass through – and wonder why it cannot remain so. But the most lost of lanes requires repair and

maintenance if it is not to revert to a mud-mired track; ditches have to be cleared to prevent flooding; hedges need to be laid so they are stockproof; and verges have to be cut if wild flowers are to flourish and brambles denied world domination.

A single lane is a nature reserve. In the wind and wet of a west country winter the sunken lane, reinforced above by a tunnel of trees and overgrown hedges, offers shelter to its banks that in spring's early warmth will light up

with snowdrops and violets, primroses and bluebells: then in summer's heat will become cool, fern-filled, dappled shade. At all seasons it will effortlessly display flower and shrub arrangements that seem miraculous to those who labour to

cultivate a natural effect in their own gardens. There are few more breathtaking sights than a roadside verge flushed with purple orchids in late spring, or

Above
Chawleigh Week Cross

a high summer hedgerow exuberant with dogrose and honeysuckle, cow pars-
ley and campion, waving grasses and clouds of meadowsweet.

Nature absorbs much that is unlovely. In the earliest Shell Guides of the
1930s John Betjeman regarded telegraph and electricity poles and their
wirescapes as a fateful sign of suburbia in the countryside. Is it familiarity that
seems to make them acceptable many decades later, or are there now so many
worse blemishes on the face of the land? Much about them is quietly pleasing:
their function as perches for birds of prey and launching zones for migrating
birds; their variations from true vertical; their gently looping wires giving
rhythm to the journey; even the umbrella of wires radiating from the single
pole which becomes the obvious place to fix a sign, stick a notice, or hang a
street lamp in the village street. At least they have the singular virtue of being
what they are. Will a future generation one day come to think just as kindly
of the communication masts that now seem to grow out of every other clump
of trees?

Many other one-time intruders have gone native. Signposts have always
been acceptable even in the most remote country. Whether their legend is an
essential aid to navigation through the intricate web of lanes or a cause of further confusion usually requires a check of the directions with the OS map. In
the luxuriance of the summer hedgerow even the striking red of the small rural
post box is barely visible, though once located its display of collection times is
a reassuring reminder of the rhythms of rural life. Most comforting of all is the
familiar red shape of the K6 telephone box. Somehow its very presence and its
deeply satisfying classical design convey just the right note of calm reassurance
in the wildest of landscapes as it does at the centre of the metropolis.

Other arrivals are less easily absorbed in the lane, but their strangeness is
somehow the more intriguing. So it is with the isolated chapel standing stark
at a cross-roads surrounded only by fields: what was it like to be a member of
the community of faith that built in such an improbable location? A recently
planted bungalow poses different questions: how did it come to command a site
with such fine views, and why did its builders think it could escape the weather
that always ensured older houses were sheltered from such exposure? Then

there are the reminders of the easily forgotten time, not necessarily long ago, when the countryside was characterised by all kinds of industrial activity; the abutments or bridge of an abandoned railway in the middle of nowhere, its line still just visible in the adjacent fields; or an overgrown canal like the improbable Bude – Holsworthy example complete with aqueduct in the wild remote country of the parish of Pancrasweek on Devon's border with Cornwall.

Rather than being seen as a burden on the local authority responsible for its maintenance, the Devon lane has a claim to be recognised as one of the county's greatest resources. It is one of those rare components of the countryside that, far from being threatened with redundancy, is increasingly valued, and not just as a highway. One of the most heartening developments of recent years has been the acknowledgement that the lane is a rich wildlife habitat: now the lanes' verges are managed with cutting regimes that allow the full glory of verge and hedgerow to flourish. Their bosky solitudes deserve to be jealously guarded, and their perambulation should remain one of the most prized of English freedoms. After all, in Devon alone there are reckoned to be nearly 10,000 miles of lanes: more than enough to ensure that even in a whole lifetime there will always be a new lane to travel down and new things to see.

Above
Farmyard, Kentisbury Barton, Exmoor

Overleaf
Greatwood Farm, Merton, early morning

Farmstead

The heart of the country is the farmstead. From its apparently random cluster of buildings flow all the skills and expertise that sustain the familiar landscape; the husbandry of animals and crops; the maintenance of hedgerows, walls and farm tracks; the management of watercourses and woodlands. But for all its vital importance, the farmstead rarely takes a high profile. Only when seen from the air or studied on large scale maps is the dominance of Devon's settlement pattern by the thick scatter of individual farms really obvious. On the ground there is the occasional farm that straddles the lane where the muddy road seems to have become part of the yard. But the typical farmstead has all the understated reticence of the west country farmer, hidden away deep down its own farm track, embowered in its own fields and woods and only announced, if at all, by a small hand-painted wooden sign in the hedge.

Down the lane to the farm the sense of secrecy and mystery that pervades the region's landscape still endures. A visit to a Devon farm usually has to be a deliberate mission rather than a casual passing-by, often involving an encounter with those watchful lookouts of this secret kingdom, collies and geese. When at last the high hedges of the lane give way to a yard, the farmstead may seem an unlikely nerve centre of rural life: to the casual observer its site may appear to have been chosen at random, its development to have been piecemeal and its organisation to be untidy, if not chaotic. But appearances are deceptive. This is a well ordered establishment that has evolved over centuries to perfect its mediating role between the farmhouse and its fields.

Far from being haphazard or primitive guesses, farmstead sites turn out to be the best possible locations for the management of their land. In the mixed farming economy of the south west, time and again they are found to occupy a mid-slope position to manage meadow and rough grazing above, summer grazing in the wetter valley bottom below and arable fields around the house.

It is the intimacy of this long established working relationship, tried and tested over many centuries, that accounts for the ineffable sense that farmsteads are at ease and belong to their landscape. And the supreme expression of this affinity is the longhouse, a building type that belongs to Dartmoor and the other uplands and moors of the south west, where people and animals are sheltered under a common roof against the hostile weather.

So perfect is the union of form and function presented by the longhouse that it stands, with some archaeological justification, as the archetype of the farmstead. Its accommodation into the upland landscape is profound and visually compelling: the sweep of its undulating thatch reflects the contours of the hillside into which it is built; massive granite boulders are its foundation stones; and there is barely a window to be seen. But more than anything it is the sharing of the common access through the cross passage by animals and humans that catches the imagination because it offers immediate identification with the long history of life in such a place. To have seen cattle tethered against the walls of the longhouse shippon in the bitter cold of a Dartmoor winter, just across the passage from where the farmer is having his tea, is to have been given the best possible insight into how this landscape has evolved.

Here there can be no fastidious pretence that mud and manure are optional in farming: rather an affirmation that they are its essence. The combination of sticky clay soils and the wet climate mean that mud is omnipresent on the west country farm, with only a brief respite in dry summers. Ted Hughes writes of the Devon farmer's everyday experience:

> I drown in the drumming ploughland, I drag up
> Heel after heel from the swallowing of the earth's mouth,
> From clay that clutches my each step to the ankle
> With the habit of the dogged grave
> > > Ted Hughes, *The Hawk in the Rain*

And, more prosaically but equally practically, manure is at the core of the small farm's pastoral and arable economy, graphically demonstrated by the presence of the dung pit at the centre of farmyard life. Dung is heavy stuff and mucking out the shippons and cowhouses, even if mechanised, is part of the hard, back-breaking routine of the farming day: little wonder that the dung pit is placed to minimise handling from the farmyard buildings onward to the fields.

This close bond between the land and its working is carried through the organisation of the whole farmstead. It is reinforced by vegetable garden and orchard immediately embowering the farmhouse and by farm buildings enfolding the yard, defending the life of the farm from the worst of the weather. Each

of the buildings has a special function in the processing, storage and nurturing activities that continue day after day, year in year out. The key building is the barn: between its great opposing double doors grain was originally threshed by hand-flailing on the oak threshing floor until the threshing machine took over in the later nineteenth century. The south west adds its own regional flavour: the hilly terrain allows bank barns to be built into the hillside so that they can be entered at ground level at the rear while the front to the yard becomes impressively two-storied with a shippon beneath.

It is only now beginning to be recognised that the buildings of the farmstead deserve as much recognition for their contribution to regional identity as the houses and cottages now celebrated as vernacular architecture. Again it is local tradition in agricultural practice that produces variations on national themes in response to local conditions. For example in the wet south west cattle shelter is essential so another speciality is the linhay, a two-storied open-fronted shelter shed with a forage store above and animal accommodation below. Similarly most west country farms include a pound house for the

making of cider in the general assemblage of stables, cart sheds and granaries commonly found elsewhere.

All this depends on the people who work the land, and the Devon farm is a small, family affair. There are the large farms that represent the historic holdings of the yeoman farmers of the medieval period but the majority of holdings are typically between 50–100 acres, reflecting their evolution from the tenant-farming system. There has never been vast wealth in such enterprises,

Page 31
Mucking out, South Ash Farm, Kings Nympton

Left
George Stoneman, Lower Skellies, Riddlecombe

Above
Making a silage clamp, Ashbury

Overleaf
The yard, Parsonage, Iddesleigh

rather they are characterised by generations of hard work by the whole family unit, sometimes with two or three families living together to sustain an often precarious grip on the economy of the farm. In this society the farmer's wife and children, the older generation, and relations were as important as the farmer himself, as were those unsung heroes, the agricultural labourers, whose lives were often miserably poor. They are easily forgotten, partly because most of their insubstantial houses have not survived.

What is left is the yeoman farmer's house and the substantial cottage. Thousands of these started life in the medieval world, originally open to the roof with a central hearth and gradually converted to two-storied houses by the insertion of floors, stairs, partitions and chimney stacks during the next century or so. In hundreds of such houses the very same thatch that was soot-blackened by smoke from the open hearth fire is still there. The medieval thatch of Devon farms is now regarded as one of Europe's most important archaeo-botanical resources for what it says about the flora and fauna of medieval England. But it is more visceral than that: poking one's head into such a roof and coming face to face with the straw that our ancestors must have seen as they looked up from their table in the open hall 600 years ago says everything necessary about human continuity in such places.

It is this sense of continuity, as much as the social and economic entity that the farmstead represents, that remains persuasive throughout history. It is not of course the same as 50 years ago when dairy and buttery, pound house, hen house and bee-boles in the orchard still represented a virtual self-sufficiency that had survived in its essential unbroken tradition since the Middle Ages. But it is still remarkably easy to feel in direct touch with that independence of spirit which was bred there and that shows itself in the character of its people generation after generation. On the domain of the small Devon farm in remote fields and woods such independence has been hard won from the wet, clinging mud and, in the face of all farming's vicissitudes, it is highly prized and fiercely defended.

Above
First furrow, Great Warham, Beaford

Field

Small stone-walled enclosures around the bare wind-swept coasts of the Penwith peninsula; close-knit fields, hedge-banks and lanes at the heart of Devon; willow-ditched water-bound solitudes over the Somerset Levels; even rare survivals of medieval open field systems at Forrabury above Boscastle in Cornwall and Braunton Great Field in Devon: this is just a sample of the rich diversity on offer in the field patterns of south west England. The English landscape almost everywhere presents such a cornucopia in a small compass that sometimes the imagination is satiated by the richness of the panorama, and there is pleasure in savouring the uniqueness of one single component. It is especially so with fields, where, once sifted out, a single enclosure is as rewarding to contemplate as the whole panoply of land stretching to the horizon and beyond.

Take one of those small fields from the Devon landscape between the rivers Taw and Torridge. It may have first caught the eye when grazing sheep or cattle were moving across its contours, or because its even texture was being steadily but dramatically transformed by the plough, grass-cutter or combine harvester into corduroy ridges of newly-turned earth, fresh-cut hay or bright-gold straw. Or perhaps it was just the tranquillity of the fully grown hay field whose grasses were being passed over by breeze and fitful sunshine to create wave after languid wave in a green inland sea. Such contemplation most engages the imagination in the low slanting light of early morning or late evening when the field's boundaries are thrown into sharp relief. Then it is possible to distinguish its outline and begin to wonder what story is told by its present configuration.

The character of an individual field deserves to be appreciated just as every single building is valued in a street, partly because the field is the basic component of landscape and also because it often has a longer history than most buildings. Its personality will have been much influenced by local topography: the lie of the land; the run of the coastline; the course of a stream, river or estuary; soil conditions; its propensity for winter flooding or summer drought; its aspect and micro-climate. But it will also reflect the work of generation after generation of farmers who have laboured over many centuries to produce food and materials to sustain an often precarious life on the land: the field that is visual delight and historical puzzle is, and always has been, primarily a working surface.

Until recently there would have been no need to champion something as commonplace as a single field, hedgerow or wood but inexorable pressure on space in these crowded islands has prompted greater awareness of much once taken for granted. No longer is it assumed that fields are the relatively modern invention of nineteenth century parliamentary enclosure suddenly superseding the medieval open field system. It is now accepted that the landscape is much older and its evolution more continuous than once thought. Pioneers of English landscape history like W G Hoskins used the evidence offered by the Devon landscape to trace the story of the field and its boundaries into the early medieval period: their successors have extended that exploration even further into prehistory, as Andrew Fleming has famously done with his work on the Dartmoor reaves.

Parallel developments in scientific understanding reinforced the discoveries of landscape history. Max Hooper was the first to examine the botanical make-up of the hedgerow: he found a correlation in centuries between the age of a hedge and the number of tree and shrub species it contains. A nineteenth century Enclosure Act hedge will typically have two, usually hawthorn and ash; an older hedge of the seventeenth century will have four; and a hedge with five or more species will probably date from the medieval period. More recent research has pointed to the evidence of trees and woodland in the history of the countryside. Oliver Rackham has shown that hedgerows can be what he evocatively calls 'the ghosts of woods', the remnants of former ancient woodlands that were grubbed out perhaps many centuries ago to leave their edges as present-day field boundaries.

Field boundaries are one of the countryside's greatest resources and Devon has a particularly rich asset in its hedgerows. Often of medieval or even

Below
Coppiced hedge and sheep, Dolton

Overleaf
Pitt Farm and the river Exe, near Cadbury

earlier origin, the typical Devon hedgerow is essentially a massive earth bank crowned by trees and shrubs. They were managed not just by laying in the traditional way to make a stock-proof fence but by coppicing to provide wood, poles and firewood for charcoal. Where hedgerow trees flourish in a pattern of small fields the country takes on the character of an open woodland with clearings, and feels like the rich flourishing habitat for local flora and fauna that it certainly is. But occasionally a single hedgerow tree in silhouette against the sky line can be compelling even in the most elegiac of landscapes.

Around the fringes of the uplands and moors and in other marginal areas there is evidence of the making of field boundaries of much more recent origin. The last great push to tame the wilderness that was undertaken by the

Above
Stonewalled enclosures, Cawsand Hill, Dartmoor

Right
Stephen Squire and Alf Pugsley laying a hedge, Langham, Dolton

great estates in the nineteenth century is often the explanation for the curiously regular stone-walled enclosures that show up so dramatically against the open moors: there are particularly clear examples on the northern flank of Dartmoor above Throwleigh and South Zeal. Of similar date are the small bulb fields on the Scilly Isles, created as an attempt by a Victorian entrepreneur to revive the economy of the islands. Some features were even imported in the face of local vernacular traditions: the stone built walls topped by beech hedges that characterise parts of Exmoor are the product of an ambitious nineteenth-century enterprise by the Knight Estate which brought in wall-building techniques from the north of England.

Lighting the pattern and texture of history is the palette of colours offered by the working of the land. The base paint is green, the subtlest and most infinitely variable colour of the landscape and, as any artist would testify, the most difficult to capture: in its early summer freshness the greenness of green seems both unsurpassable and unforgettable. Under the plough soil colours are revealed; brown loams, yellow grey clays, thin chalky whites, jet black peat, vivid red sandstone. As the year progresses field colours track the seasons, peaking in the defining colours of high summer: in a good harvest the rich unburnished golds of ripening cereals against azure blue skies are transformed by the combine into stubble and straw of shining gold: in a bad summer the same fields will be black with the rotting crop. And then there are the exotics that joyfully protest at any tendency to reduce the English landscape to tasteful pastel tones: the acid yellow of oil seed rape may be difficult to take in some lights but the prospect of an improbably powder-blue field of flax in full sun, especially with a dash of red poppies, is journey-stopping.

Ancient farmsteads that have enjoyed continuity of stewardship if not ownership may still possess a map of the farm hanging somewhere of importance in the farmhouse that shows all the fields and their boundaries. Each enclosure will have its own name that will reflect its function, size and character, a name that will often have survived many changes of tenant or landlord. Reading field names on such maps or in farm inventories conveys the most vivid sense of the quiet intimacy that belongs to the English landscape, springing from many centuries of cultivation that have established the distinctive personality of each small parcel of land. It is a reminder that each easy view has been created over thousands of years through the enduring union between what earth has given and human hands have made.

Left
Fields and the river Torridge, Torrington

Above
Orchard with sheep, Whimple

Orchard

Scilly Pearl and Lady's Finger. Cornish Aromatic, Gilliflower and Plympton King. Devonshire Quarrendon, Crimson Costard, Sweet Coppin, Michaelmas Stubbard, Slack ma Girdle, Tremlett's Bitter and Sweet Alford. Camelot, Cheddar Cross, Beauty of Bath, Hoary Morning, Lambrook Pippin, Harry Master's Jersey and Dunkerton Late Sweet. Names like these, just a few of the more than six thousand known varieties of apple, belong to the orchards of the west country. They gently but sturdily voice their local provenance in soft burred local dialects from Scilly to Somerset, deep rooted on the farms where they were first recognised, living testimony to the skill of the local people who first grafted them. Just to read their names is to instantly recall the promise of their springtime blossoms, the scent of their ripening aromas hanging in the autumn air, and arouse a thirst for those sunlit ciders that evoke the personality of a peninsula once one of the greatest apple growing areas in the world.

At the beginning of the twentieth century, a large-scale map of most of Devon shows an orchard-embowered world. Apple orchards predominate, although some localities had other specialities: Thorverton was celebrated for its wall fruits, particularly its apricots, Dittisham for its plums and damsons, and Atherington and Landkey for their Mazzard cherries. Every farm had its own orchard, lowland farmers commonly planting and maintaining large acreages but even upland farmsteads usually had a few trees in the vegetable garden. Substantial acreages of apple orchards endure as a significant component of the south west landscape. They frame the sky for many miles across the Somerset Levels. Commercial cider orchards flourish in the Vale of Taunton and can still be recognised in the Whimple area of east Devon even if the huge white letters that emerge from among the apple trees now advertise a local antiques dealer rather than Whiteways cider. And in sheltered valleys leading down to the sea on the south coast of Devon and Cornwall there are many survivors from the time, only a few decades ago, when orchard blossom was reckoned one of the great sights that spring visitors came to see.

The planting of orchards in Britain is now thought to go back to Anglo-Saxon and probably Roman times. Cider was certainly noted as a regular part of the dietary regime of the south west in manorial accounts of the medieval

period, the fruit being grown in what is evocatively described as 'the apple garden'. About 1600 John Hooker refers to the painstaking cultivation of orchards and abundance of fruit in Devon and by 1754 the author of *The Compleat Cyderman* records that Devon surpassed all other counties in the management of fruit trees, skills in grafting, and the production of new varieties. But perhaps the most telling account is William Marshall's disapproving assessment of 1806:

'Not withstanding the accumulation of evils arising from the production, use and abuse of cider, the men of Devon are more strongly attracted to it than

Left
Ronnie Huxtable picking apples, Harracott

Above
Bagged cider apples, near Glastonbury

even those of Herefordshire. Their Orchards might well be styled their Temples and Apple Trees their Idols of Worship'.

To contemplate an old orchard of standard trees with tall trunks and broad canopies, even if some are fallen but still productive, is to people the imagination with generations of countrymen and women whose lives were refreshed and enriched – and, in fairness to Marshall, sometimes ruined – by what has traditionally been described as 'the principal liquor' of the west of England. Not only was it the main drink for the farmer's own social purposes, it was directly employed in the relationship between the farmer and his labour force as a form of wage known as 'cider truck'. Despite its abolition by law in 1887, farmers continued to believe that they had to provide good cider to attract good labour right up until the Second World War. Large quantities were required: men were entitled to 2 quarts a day, boys to 1, with prodigious amounts consumed at harvest time.

Cider evolved into one of the most distinctive local industries, different varieties of apple, soil conditions and production methods being reflected in unique local ciders. Some areas were particularly renowned for their cider fruit: in Somerset around Wedmore, Glastonbury, Baltonsborough, Taunton and Martock, in Devon the South Hams: W G Hoskins gives us a mouth-watering description of Totnes cider 'which, like a golden vin du pays, solaces the historical traveller all over this part of Devon'. One tradition had apples collected and stored in apple lofts because it was believed this improved their flavour. In other places the apples were left to fall and ripen on the ground for the same reason, the spread of crimson and gold over the cider orchard floor, luminous in the half-light like a Samuel Palmer painting, surely offering one of the greatest of autumn's many glories. The cider making process of crushing, pressing and storing in barrels took place in the pound house, a specialist building of the farmstead whose importance is belied by its anonymous appearance except its lack of windows: inside of course it is instantly recognisable if the great cider press is still in place.

Orchards always offered more than cider. The height, spread and generous spacing of standard trees allows grazing of the grass beneath the canopy

Above
Orchard with mistletoe, Kingsbury Episcopi

Overleaf
Orchard, St Dominick

by cattle, sheep, pigs and poultry. Interplanting, particularly with potatoes, was noted as one of the advantages of orchard cultivation by eighteenth- and nineteenth-century observers. Bee hives were always found there because bees were considered essential for pollination: the blossom offered an invaluable source of pollen for bee colonies to thrive on and to produce surplus honey in good years. Another traditional, if accidental, crop is mistletoe with its orangey-green lanterns that hang in the bare trees and glow against the winter sky. All this is bound together in the interdependent world of animals, birds, insects and plants that orchards sustain. And the wood of the fruit tree can even enjoy a sweet after-life, apple wood being sought after for its hardness and so traditionally employed for the cogs of mill machinery, while plum, pear and cherry are valued for their colour in fine furniture inlays.

It comes hard to face the tragedy of orchard destruction that has happened in recent years. Only 30 years ago Devon and Somerset each still had the second largest acreage of orchards in England behind Herefordshire: they have lost over 90% of that area since then. Orchards came to be seen as unproductive parts of the farmstead, their destruction officially sanctioned with grubbing-up grants until as late as 1988. Even worse, any orchard within a hamlet or village was eagerly bought up for its potential to grow houses instead of trees. In the south western landscape where the pattern of settlement is generally so loosely woven, the loss of an old orchard somehow tautens the weave so that the characteristic generosity of layout, creating a place at ease with itself, is gradually lost.

A fight-back is underway. New orchards are being planted, old varieties rescued, real apples with bite and flavour becoming available again. As yet these are only small beginnings, but they gladden the heart because somehow the orchard matters above most such things. It is partly its gentle amiability, nicely conveyed by those bird's-eye views of the great houses and estates of the seventeenth and eighteenth centuries where their owners and guests are often shown walking and talking companionably in the orchard. And there is its enduring symbolism in human affairs as a rich source of artistic and spiritual inspiration: even the biblical account of paradise in Genesis uses the fruit tree in the garden as its most potent image – and that itself is borrowed from Greek and

Persian antecedents. So it has continued into our own age: right at the climax of his mystical journeyings in *Four Quartets*, T S Eliot chooses to write of:

> the children in the apple tree
> Not known, because not looked for
> But heard, half-heard, in the stillness
> Between two waves of the sea.
>
> T S Eliot, *Little Gidding*

Here again the orchard stands as symbol of the earthly paradise that offers in its timeless moment the intersection of time and eternity.

Vegetable Garden

There is no better way to form first impressions of unfamiliar country, or revisit a landscape beloved and longed for, than to travel by train and savour the view from the window. At high speed there is the exhilaration of broad panoramas that unfold like summer clouds in never ending succession. Whenever the train slows, it is the detail that is engaging, even near the heart of the city or through the seemingly endless suburbs. And in the countryside there is special pleasure to be had on the branch lines, of which there are few more delectable in the south west than the journey into north Devon from Exeter to Barnstaple. Houses turn their backs on railways and so the rail traveller is offered a continuous version of a walk down a village street on a winter's afternoon before the curtains have been drawn, when glimpses of that more intimate world behind the public front are fleetingly on offer. From the train there is more than the lighted room to see: this is the back garden world of sheds and washing lines, the odd fruit tree, grass mown to perfection or gone to wilderness, the greenhouse and the vegetable patch.

With the notable exception of allotment society, urban life firmly dictates that vegetable gardens belong to the private rather than the public domain. In the countryside their public profile is higher, partly perhaps because privacy has not until recently been at such a premium: here vegetables are commonly visible from the village street, over a wall or through a hedge, next to the churchyard or simply giving on to neighbouring fields. In the re-invented cottage garden – what Edward Hyams famously called Jekyllism – vegetables are supposed to mingle unselfconsciously with flowers. But in the traditional rural

Left
Percy Shaxton's shallots, Noplace, Ebberley, Roborough

economy it was, and often still remains, a simple fact of life that food production needed to take priority. Vegetables will greet the visitor beside the path to the front door if there they can enjoy the best aspect for cultivation, perhaps because it is the most sheltered and favoured spot in the garden.

Vegetable plots still occupy some of the prime sites in the countryside, as sure a tribute to the significance of vegetables in rural society as the prodigious

specimens on display at the annual show. The necessity for near self-sufficiency in food production has survived surprisingly strongly in the countryside in the face of inducements like the so-called 'global summer' which sounds enticing enough until its absurdities emerge. Is a jaded palate or the elimination of delight in the delicious taste of the first new potato, strawberry and apple in season really such an achievement; or has not clever marketing simply blocked out any contact with nature's rhythms and disciplines? However small the plot,

Left
Vegetable garden, early morning, Langham, Dolton

Above
Reuben Clements selecting entries for the Flower Show, Dolton

Overleaf
Vegetable garden, Merton

growing a few vegetables demands commitment to a particular patch of earth and exposure to the vicissitudes of the weather throughout the year.

There is something to see on the vegetable plot even on the worst day of winter. Even if the high hopes of summer still lie where they fell after the first frosts there will be the comfort and dependability of winter greens and the sleeping promise of the bare earth. Digging over the plot instantly changes its appearance, the colour of the newly turned earth fresh and strong, a microcosm of the larger endeavour undertaken in the ploughed fields of the wider landscape. The same basic good husbandry is demanded year on year: the supreme test is whether by late spring the soil can be brought to a fine tilth, that state of near mythical perfection demanded by the instructions on the back of the seed packet, ready for successful sowing.

Soon after come the early summer mornings when a daily inspection will reveal the first shoots showing amazing rates of growth. As the crops grow on, are weeded, thinned or planted out they weave their different patterns, textures and colours over the ground. This is the season when the polite gardener's assertion that vegetables could possibly look good if only they were not planted in rows can be triumphantly countered. Earth has hardly anything to show more fair than a well-tended vegetable plot in early summer with rows of root crops, newly earthed-up potatoes and exuberantly climbing peas and beans. And when in late summer the runner beans are a scrambling mass of scarlet flowers and long green pods; when marrows are swelling to culinary uselessness but irresistible harvest-festival hugeness; when onions are ripening in ordered perfection; when the first potatoes are lifted; then the early promise seems fulfilled beyond any reasonable expectation.

Writ large the individual vegetable plot becomes the society of the allotment. It is curious how allotments are often regarded as an exclusively urban phenomenon. They date from the land enclosure that began in earnest in the

Right
Michael Mitchell in his garden, Dolton

eighteenth century when whole sections of rural society were made landless: the allotment offered some small compensation. Allotments occasionally became a major political issue in the nineteenth century, resulting in considerable acreages being provided in the major cities to which the rural poor had fled. But it was not just the city that showed up the worst extremes of poverty and wealth: most contemporary descriptions of the countryside in the eighteenth and nineteenth centuries stressed the wretchedness of much rural life. Rural cottages were often landlocked so the allotment became as important a part of the fabric of rural communities as it ever was in towns.

In many parts of the south west small plots for growing food and in good years producing a small surplus that could be sold in the local market were an essential insurance against the vagaries of precarious employment. This was as true of the mining communities as it was of the fishing villages: both are often surrounded by a network of miniature fields on the more sheltered slopes around the settlement, often still discernible even if now neglected and overgrown. They take on a uniquely distinctive character on the Isles of Scilly where small strips of land sheltered by walls and hedges are used to grow early flowers and vegetables, giving exactly the right scale and definition to this most intimate of landscapes. On the mainland, traces of the formerly flourishing horticultural enterprises can still be found around the lower Tamar Valley. In such intermediate stages the food production chain that starts with the individual vegetable plot eventually merges into the farmed landscape.

Perhaps because they so directly encapsulate a sense of belonging, vegetable gardens seem to represent one of the roots of a sane and stable society. No surprise then to find them disregarded and instead seen as ideal parcels of land for development through that most innocuous-sounding but deadly of post-war planning policies, infilling. This means that every small gap of open land or over-large garden; each secret cob-walled plot; those unkempt allotments with their gently anarchic culture; that handful of small fields; will all be seen as potential building sites. The results are distressingly obvious in almost every rural settlement, however remote. It is not just the vitality of the soil that is destroyed, whose quality may have been built up for generations, but the vitality and distinctiveness of the whole place.

Infilled settlements look as though they have had the life squeezed out of them. Spaces between and around buildings are just as much part of the character that defines one place as different from another as its geography, street pattern, buildings and trees. From the top of the local church tower this interplay of spaces and structures is wonderfully visible. From here it is clear how slowly and organically the settlement has grown over the last thousand years, and also how rapid has been later twentieth-century development. And if a count is made of all the vegetable plots visible from this unique vantage point – adding in a few secret plots as well as the allotments – it will be only too obvious what would happen to the *genius loci* if they were all built over. It is time to give vegetable gardens the recognition, honour and protection so long overdue and so richly deserved.

Above
Cob shed, near Burrington

Overleaf
Cob barns, Broomham, Kings Nympton

Cob

It seemed to have always been there, that small building in the corner of the field clearly visible through the bare hedge in winter. With the passing years it became an old friend, part of the familiar landscape whose presence was reassuring even if its existence was taken for granted during its leafy summer seclusion. On the rare occasions when it drew a closer look, its slightly shabby well-worn appearance served only to enhance its personality, with more than a few missing slates and sheets of corrugated iron not quite covering the holes. And it was heartening to see that it was still used as a field shelter long after its original function – barn, linhay or cottage perhaps – had been forgotten. Then one winter, after a bad gale or heavy snowfall, part of the roof caved in to expose the wall tops to the weather and allow the rain to soak the walls right through. Another year or so and the raw earth of its construction began to turn to mud and spill down to the ground. Now it is slipping slowly but inexorably back to earth again, to rejoin the mud of the neighbouring lanes, fields and farmsteads.

Such small histories must have been rehearsed over and over again during more than 5,000 years of human occupation in south west England, leaving behind not even the memory of lumps or bumps in fields but adding to the mystery of what is known in this part of the world simply as cob. To the exile from Devon the very word resonates with images of home, instantly calling to mind softly moulded buildings sitting comfortably among rounded hills, small fields and orchards, red soils, warm enclosure, timelessness. The derivation of this short simple word is unknown, cob being the regional dialect name for the mud wall that is elsewhere in England variously called clunch in East Anglia, wychert in Buckinghamshire and clay daubin on the Solway Plain. But nowhere in England is there so much mud building as there is in Devon, where cob

Below
Remains of cob wall, Broomham, Kings Nympton

Right
Cob barn, Narracott, Hollocombe

has its national heartland and from which it spreads westwards throughout Cornwall and eastwards into adjacent parts of Somerset and Dorset.

Until the awakening of interest in local building traditions of recent years the abundance of cob in the west country was almost universally interpreted as evidence of the backwardness and isolation of the peninsula. After all, other parts of England developed sophisticated timber-framed construction, a technique that is startlingly absent from the countryside of this area. But this is to

under-rate the technical excellence of earth walling in general, which has a world-wide provenance, and cob in particular. The combination of a first rate raw material in the local soils and the perfection of local building traditions over centuries made cob the pre-eminent building material for much of Devon throughout the whole period from the fourteenth to the nineteenth centuries. It was during this time that the bulk of the county's domestic historic building stock was constructed and cob was employed right across the social range for everything from the humblest farm shelter to the most prestigious yeoman farmer's house. By itself cob is virtually undateable but when other features of west-country houses, especially their roof carpentry, are considered it is possible to claim with certainty that there is a vast amount of medieval cob in Devon.

Cob building traditions were hard won. Mud cracks when it dries and this can mean structural failure if the whole building is made of it. The local builders of more than 500 years ago may have started with soils that were less

likely to shrink dramatically while drying – partly because they contained a natural aggregate called shillet – but only local tradition could determine what the right mix was, how much straw needed to be added to bind the cob and further minimise the shrinkage problem, or whether any additional aggregate was required. The wet mass of newly mixed cob is dense and intractable, heavy work in itself, but it then has to be pitched up on to the top of an ever heightening wall where it has to be tamped and trodden down to compact it. Each layer or raise then has to be left to dry before the next layer can be added, a slow and labour-intensive process that is forever afterwards discernible in the

Left
The Barton, Sheepwash

Above
Cob roundhouse, Rudge Farm, Lapford

horizontal lines of an unrendered wall. It is worth pausing sometimes before an apparently commonplace section of cob to reflect both on the skill of its builders and also on how many hundreds of hours of back-breaking human labour are represented there.

Each cob wall can truly be called unique because it will represent the fusion of a very localised building material – soil that has been dug from the site where it was to be used – with the local technique for building with it, one of the clearest expressions of a vernacular tradition anywhere in England. And that uniqueness will be enhanced by time. Protected by a stone plinth below and, originally at least, a generous eaves overhang above, unrendered cob will show in its rounded corners and deepened surface textures its conversation with the local weather that began on the day it was built. On such weather-beaten surfaces the low light of morning or evening plays delightfully to show up the constituent materials: soil, shillet and straw, a landscape in miniature, a vertical ploughed field, inviting to the eye and to the touch. Similarly, although thousands of cob buildings are disguised behind a coat of lime render, the render was repeatedly lime washed, producing a patina with ageing that when caught by slanting light seems to shimmer with the undulations of the centuries.

'Earth to earth' is the phrase that often comes to mind when contemplating the unison of cob and its landscape, so deep-rooted and natural is the relationship. And nothing so perfectly expresses this as the colours of cob: deep reds, rich ochres and yellows, pale creams, warm browns and even cold greys, they endure in the memory of landscapes otherwise only half-remembered. It is because cob walls hold the earth in common with their fields and therefore the buildings change colour with the soils that they seem to belong more effortlessly to their landscapes than even the most perfect stone-built houses. And the colours are always changing, subtly responding to local conditions even in areas of apparently uniform soils. Sometimes the changes are striking, especially where the complicated geology of the south west collides with itself to produce dramatic contrasts of soils within the space of a few miles. The best place to see this is in Devon to the north and west of Crediton where red and yellow cob intermingles throughout that deep, lost countryside.

Only a few years ago cob was tottering gently into an esoteric section of English provincial history but recently it has experienced an unexpected renaissance. Cob is now found on the agenda of planning committees and its construction and repair are the subject of student dissertations, research projects, conferences and even television documentaries. Pamphlets are available, learned articles continue to be written, and at least one hard-back handbook has been published. Even better, new cob buildings are being constructed in Devon: first the now locally celebrated bus shelter at Down St Mary and more recently extensions to existing buildings and completely new houses. And it seems only yesterday that building societies magisterially refused mortgages on cob buildings because they were self-evidently little better than peasant hovels liable to return to mud as soon as the rainy season started.

There are some nice ironies here. Each new age has a natural and understandable tendency to discard tradition because of the promise of the new, but how did we come to lose centuries of building tradition so suddenly and almost irreversibly? The process by which cob building has had to be rediscovered has been a salutary corrective to the notion that late twentieth-century technology and expertise can solve everything, especially something as primitive as building a mud wall. As with so much that disappears before its true value has been appreciated, cob has proved humblingly resistant to slick reinvention: instead it has had to be learned laboriously all over again by making the same mistakes it took previous generations centuries to overcome.

Above
Corrugated iron shed, Fordton, Crediton

Corrugated Iron

There come days after the first frosts of every autumn when drying grass and dying bracken so burnish Devon's uplands and moors that the hills glow even in the gloom of an equinoctial gale and if caught in strong slanting sunlight against a sky of battleship grey they blaze in russets and golds. Each such moment is unique in the infinite play of light on landscape, delighting the eye and satisfying the senses through the union of human activity and the natural world in the colours and textures of common land and enclosure, field boundaries and farmsteads, buildings and landscape. Only when we focus more sharply on the individual buildings of the farmstead might we realise we have naturally absorbed into this palette of harmonious perfection some rusted roofs of corrugated iron.

Yet 'corrugated' as it is generally and affectionately known does not always have a good press and is sometimes even depicted as an undesirable alien in the countryside. At worst this is the prejudice that sees it belonging in the slums and shanty towns of the global village but not for that very reason in the 'heritage landscape'. At best it is an emblem of stereotyped rusticity from which quasi-peasant wretchedness the incomer can offer deliverance; Flora Post's serial cleanup at Cold Comfort Farm must surely have included a purge of every sheet of corrugated about the place. Almost all references to this material assume it to be a tawdry twentieth-century introduction that has tarnished the countryside's natural thatched innocence.

The facts of its history are rather different. Corrugated iron was invented and patented in Britain as early as the 1820s and was the first mass-produced cladding material of the modern building industry. By 1850 it was being used with iron and timber frames for prefabricated buildings manufactured here and exported all over the world. It was a technological breakthrough. The corrugations give strength and considerable structural advantages over flat sheeting, even allowing it to be built in a curved profile as a self-supporting barrel roof to cover relatively large areas. So it is that the same material cladding the humblest woodshed on a remote Devon smallholding was taken up by kings, princes and governors: as early as 1843 in Africa King Eyambo of Calabar chose corrugated from a Liverpool firm to clad his sumptuous new iron palace for himself and his 320 wives. It was subsequently to be employed in cathedrals, churches and chapels; dockyards, barracks and

warehouses; town halls, offices and shops; villas and cottages, sheds and shelters throughout the remotest parts of Empire and to the uttermost parts of the earth.

It soon became a familiar feature of the British landscape. In 1861 J B Denton wrote in the *Journal of the Royal Agricultural Society of England* '*On the comparative cheapness and advantages of iron and wood in the construction of roofs of farm buildings*'. It was especially useful for roofing some of the large Victorian farming enterprises that were even then known as factory farms. They must

Left
Corrugated cow shed, Langham, Dolton

Above
Gates at Millhams, Dolton

Overleaf
Barns, Higher Hacknell, Burrington

have seemed strange newcomers: the spectacular example at Eastwood Manor Farm, East Harptree in Somerset completed in 1858 looks like a railway terminus absent-mindedly erected in the middle of the Mendips from which a steam train might emerge at any moment. On the more traditional farm prefabricated buildings became increasingly popular as manufacturers' catalogues offered corrugated iron dairies, stables, lambing sheds, shepherds' huts, cottages, rickstands and rickcovers.

For over a century the archetype of prefabrication on the farm has been the Dutch barn. Although indisputably a newer arrival in the family of traditional farm buildings this is a structure that seems comfortably settled into the farmstead cluster. Its modest scale relates well to the older ranges and can even mitigate the impact of much larger late twentieth century buildings by providing a transition in scale and materials between the vernacular and the contemporary. Standing alone in the fields it displays an intrinsic elegance, its slender steel uprights supporting the gentle convex curve of its roof sometimes echoed in the rhythm of the curved-headed bracing between the bays. Stuffed

Left
Boulton and Paul barn near Winkleigh

Above
Combine and Nissen hut, Hollocombe

with yellow bales after harvest it offers even the casual passer-by a reassuring guarantee that provision has been made against the coming winter.

Low cost and general utility ensure that corrugated has always found employment in the various repair jobs that need doing on the farm. Its lightness means that it can be used to re-roof farmyard buildings on the existing roof carpentry without expensive structural alterations. Its replacement of costly or unobtainable thatch, slate or clay tiles is undoubtedly a loss of that sense of naturally belonging in the landscape which is effortlessly displayed by vernacular roofing traditions. But how much more catastrophic would have been the wholesale disappearance of the buildings themselves. It is no exaggeration to acclaim corrugated a hero of the countryside because for well over a century it has prevented the otherwise inexorable decay of unroofed cob or earth-mortared rubble walls in the pervasive wetness of the south west's weather. Through the seemingly inevitable cycles of relative prosperity, recession and downright despair that are the lot of the farming community it has saved the familiar buildings of the farmstead from certain dereliction.

In the long established rural version of design-and-build, corrugated is the stuff of improvisation for roofing over the yard, lean-to extensions, field shelters, sheds and mended fences. Its curved virtuosity is ingeniously deployed as the coping to cob walls and even as canopies over the pointed-headed windows of a Methodist chapel proud of its rustic Gothick. With a little imagination a Nissen hut's prefabricated portability allows it to become almost anything on the farm; and a garage, scout hut or village hall elsewhere. Sadly, natural rust-red, which looks so at home against a Dartmoor landscape of dried bracken or a ploughed field of red Devon soil, is evidence of corrosion. Corrugated must be painted even if galvanised but fortunately paint not only enhances durability but almost always visual attraction as well. Bituminous black is traditional and always looks well in the landscape but the heart often rejoices in bold essays in blue, green and red that give points of colour and protest against a soulless tastefulness.

Its supremacy was eventually challenged in the late 1930s by the introduction of asbestos cement sheeting which offered better insulation and required no maintenance but whose corrugations are too wide and whose colour is anaemic compared to the original. More modern competitors have emerged with better colours but still wider corrugations. Nevertheless the original and best, now usually called 'galvanised', lives healthily on. Officialdom, at least in the form of the Ministry of Agriculture, has proved reluctant to accept its unpretentious virtues for the repair of traditional buildings. There is an indisputable case for its widespread use not only in the conservation of existing structures but in their sympathetic extension and sometimes at least for the wholly new.

In the nineteenth century the detractors of corrugated iron inevitably included the ecclesiastical establishment who mocked the catalogue chapels of nonconformity as 'tin tabernacles'. Methodism soon shattered such presumption by demonstrating how humble temporary buildings could serve the spiritual needs of ever changing mining communities in the far south west better than the ancient parish churches stranded by their medieval geography in the wrong place. In the wastes, noise and dirt of the mining areas the 'tin tent' of the chapel must indeed have seemed like a sanctuary in the wilderness. Anyone caught out in the worst of weathers will have known at least faint echoes of such experience when refuge is sought under the roof of a field barn and the rain drums deafeningly on the tin and a loose sheet bangs in the wind; we have been offered all we needed, no more and no less. That is what corrugated has always offered. It has entered the soul of the countryside in countless different guises and has long since proved it belongs there.

Above
Spoil heap, Carluddon, near St Austell

Overleaf
Spoil heap and quarry, Stenalees, St Austell

Quarry

Of all the excitements of the journey westward there is nothing quite like the first glimpse of the china clay waste tips around St Austell. Jutting ragged across the horizon they shine and glint startlingly white like an improbable mountain range in the quiet green landscape of mid Cornwall. But these man-made hills are not alien intruders: at the very least they have a better claim to belong to Cornwall than many later newcomers because they are the present representatives of the extractive industries that have so profoundly shaped Cornish history. They are the source of so much of its wealth as well as its endemic poverty, the builder of many of its townscapes and the moulder of large tracts of its landscape. Now that the last Cornish tin mine has finally closed these most westerly working waste tips stand as powerful symbols of the pervasive influence of such ancient industries in the history of the west of England.

Yet today the very mention of mining or quarrying is enough to arouse splenetic letters to the newspapers and hefty petitions to the local planning authority. The china clay industry of Lee Moor and the great limestone quarries at Meldon on western Dartmoor are now often seen as inappropriate activities for a National Park, despite the continuous industrial history of the moor. Strong opposition is fully justified when what is proposed involves large-scale incursions into modest landscapes, like the giant bites that the roadstone quarries have made into Somerset's gentle Mendips. These vast multinational enterprises threaten our blue remembered hills, and so come to represent the forces of destruction that always seem waiting in the wings to ruin the cherished local scene.

But for centuries there have also been hundreds of small quarries in the countryside that provided employment and building materials for little more than their immediate locality. In the sum of small things that make one place different from another it is arguably the products of the local quarry used in walls and roofs, pavings and field boundaries, that matter most: there is something engaging about

the immediacy of using materials from near at hand for local building, and something enthralling too. To visit the smallest quarry is to enter a world of strange awesome beauty; where the rock is laid bare in huge raw exposures; where machines seem reduced to the scale of toys; where deep pools of silent water lie at the bottom of the pit. Here are genuine drama and excitement in the noise and dirt, and more than a hint of danger. But how easily all this is forgotten. Once back

on the surface, the visual delights of local stone walls and slate roofs showing off their textures and colours in farmhouses, hamlets and small towns quickly erase memories of their messy birth.

Even in the medieval period some building materials were considered so prestigious that they were transported hundreds of miles to embellish churches and cathedrals, manors and country houses. As early as the thirteenth century slates from the Kingsbridge area of south Devon were exported in large quantities by sea for the King's Works all over southern England. In the fourteenth century Fabric Rolls of Exeter Cathedral we can read how its great rebuilding was achieved

Left
Disused quarry, Merrivale, Dartmoor

Above
Newbridge quarry, Dolton

Below
Les Bryant breaking rocks, Newbridge, Dolton

Right
Delabole slate quarry

with stone from at least fourteen Devon quarries as well as from Hameldon in Somerset, Purbeck in Dorset and Caen in Normandy. The quarries from which these materials came can usually still be traced and exercise a powerful hold on the imagination. Standing on top of the cliffs east of Salcombe Regis in east Devon, it is possible to picture the scene 600 years ago as the stone from the still-visible faces nearby was lowered to the beach to be transported by sea up the Exe estuary for the walls of the new Cathedral.

But until the canal and railway age the cost of transport was prohibitive except for such sumptuous projects. Local provenance was usually all important, as on thousands of west country farms where stone must have been quarried on site at least for rubble walling if not for display features such as door surrounds and fireplaces. The availability and quality of materials influenced the evolution of local building traditions in all kinds of subtle ways: for example slate roofs in Cornwall and west Devon show a clear distinction between the rag slate tradition – the very large slates available in north Cornwall – and the scantle slate technique of smaller slates laid in random widths and diminishing courses employed over the rest of the area. And when mason and slater had completed what the quarryman had begun, it was the turn of the local weather over the years to enhance the newly exposed surfaces with patinas and textures and encourage lichens to add patterns and colours never even dreamed of by the builder.

The disappearance of smaller quarries – even that most visible of Dartmoor quarries at Merrivale on the Tavistock–Princetown road has now closed – reflects the standardisation of building materials that has accelerated the decline of regional identity. While we struggle to keep open a few British slate quarries, cheaper slate is imported from as far afield as China and South America. But there are some signs that the tide may be turning at last. New supplies of traditional materials are always needed just to repair existing buildings, otherwise conserva-tion ends up as a futile exercise of robbing other old buildings to provide them; many a farmstead has lost its slate roofs to the lucrative trade in second-hand slates. As a result, ancient quarries like Delabole in north Cornwall, which is known to have supplied slates for the building of prestigious developments like Bridgeland Street in Bideford in the seventeenth century, have in recent years been given a new lease of life.

This has inspired the beginnings of a concerted effort to reopen old quarries and search for new ones. But any development in the countryside which smacks of destruction is bound to be fiercely resisted, however worthy the cause, and such initiatives have often run into local opposition. This was graphically demonstrated during the 1980s when the very limited reworking of one small face of the Salcombe Regis quarries was proposed for a major repair programme at Exeter Cathedral: even though the amount of stone required was almost negligible com-mercially – less than 80 tons a year for 10 years – the matter had to go to a public inquiry before being decided in the Cathedral's favour. Attitudes are changing. English Heritage, the government's statutory advisor on conservation issues, now campaigns for the use of local building materials with posters showing working quarries and the slogan 'English Heritage wants to see more eyesores like this'.

Quarries of this local scale offer so much that we need, a means of earthing new building into our localities and a way of ensuring that the countryside can pro-vide employment and so be sustained as a working environment. And even after their resources of usable stone and slate have been exhausted, abandoned quarries become compelling and intriguing places, rich wildlife habitats with geological exposures that are often protected as Sites of Special Scientific Interest. Such places exercise a strange power even if we only know them as evocative names on the map; Catacleuse from Cataclews Point high on the cliffs beyond Padstow; Polyphant on the eastern edge of Bodmin Moor; Serpentine on the Lizard; Hurdwick near Tavistock; Haytor on Dartmoor; Raddon west of Thorverton; Beer on the white cliffs where Devon meets Dorset; Lundy Island granite. From these unlikely, often inaccessible, locations have come the raw materials for some of the finest and highest of architectural endeavour all over the west of England and beyond.

Above
Graveyard and chapel, Aller Bridge, Coldridge

Chapel

Chapel country is distinctive, leaner in its landscape, starker in its townscape. The rural chapel is likely to be happened-upon in the village street, on the outskirts of a settlement down a steep lane, or at a country cross-roads surrounded only by fields. The urban chapel is more prominent, characteristic of the industrial settlements that suddenly sprawled across the landscape in the nineteenth century. Its building style is difficult to categorise, only rarely hitting the architectural big-time even in the major towns and cities. And instead of a dedication to St Mary, St Michael the Archangel, the apostles, or even a local saint, the roundel on its front will proclaim it to be Bethel, Beulah, Mount Sion, Reheboah, Salem or Shiloh, somehow redolent of another, older religion.

That church and chapel feel different reflects their distinctive history and culture. While the parish church has been part of English society for a thousand years, the chapel is strongly, though by no means exclusively, connected to a neglected section of English social and economic history, the industrial history of the countryside – and has too often been treated as if it was as transitory as the buildings, machinery, spoil-heaps and settlements of the industrial landscape. In the south west it is already difficult to find obvious traces of the Bristol and north Somerset coal-fields that were still working in the 1960s. The ancient metalliferous mining industries of the Mendips, Dartmoor and Exmoor are now more archaeology than history. Only in Cornwall has the story of the extractive industries been recognised as valuable in its own right, rather than something to be expunged as unworthy from the cultural consciousness.

Dissent, to use the older term for religious groups outside the Anglican church, already had deep roots in the south west by the seventeenth century, flourishing especially in east Devon on the strength of the textile industry. But the spectacular revival of what the Victorians called Nonconformity was fuelled by the failure of the established church to comprehend how radically the economy and society of the south west was changed by the vast expansion of mining industries in west Devon and Cornwall in the first half of the nineteenth century. John Wesley's message of redemption from the travails of the grim, often dangerous lives of the miner, agricultural worker or fisherman to a glorious future life, allied with social action to mitigate poverty, insecurity and sickness, was direct and persuasive. The culture of Dissent runs deep in the west country, grafted on to the independence of spirit that has always found expression in the region's politics: this is country that has never been completely seduced by the mainstream orthodoxies, whatever they were currently labelled.

Whatever Wesley, himself a good Anglican, intended, chapel life came to represent the culture of the outsider. It was an alternative society, whose membership risked social exclusion and even legal sanction from the establishment, but in which the humblest could rise to become leaders, teachers and pastors. Nonconformity embraced the whole range of religious experience from the quiet contemplation of the Society of Friends to the countless local revivals

Left
Chapel and schoolroom, Hollocombe

Below
Harvest Festival decorations, Congregational chapel, Chulmleigh

Overleaf
Zion Methodist chapel, Riddlecombe, Ashreigney

and enthusiasms of the Wesleyans. The earliest meetings took place in a room in an ordinary cottage, probably under suspicion from neighbours. Communities evolved in various make-shift venues, sometimes taking out the floor of a cottage, frequently having a mobile chapel of corrugated iron on wheels in case there was local opposition. Eventually they felt confident enough to build a permanent chapel, though they were often still relegated to relatively remote locations.

What emerged was as diverse in its spirituality as in its buildings. At its simplest, as in the tiny Methodist chapel at Penrose in north Cornwall, or the Friends' Meeting House at evocatively named Come-to-Good in south Cornwall, the spiritual power of the buildings is as compelling as the richest and most ancient cathedral. The seating is plain pine benches in front of a small modest table with just one step up to the platform or pulpit for leader or preacher, and hardly anything else apart from a vase of hedgerow flowers, a harmonium and a row of hat-pegs. In such places the experience recorded in the old Quaker hymn still seems valid:

> Drop thy still dews of quietness
> Till all our strivings cease
> Take from our souls the strain and stress
> And let our ordered lives confess
> The beauty of thy peace.

Such sentiments must have had a special resonance in the noise, dirt and danger of the mining industry: they are powerfully evoked by such buildings as the humble corrugated iron chapel that still survives cheek-by-jowl with the quarry at Merrivale on Dartmoor.

Not all Nonconformist history, like all other religious history, is so attractive. Alongside genuine experience of lives transformed and faithful witness, there were all too frequently rivalries, disputes and schisms, and there must

Left
Clifford Strongman playing the harmonium, Penrose chapel

have been some congregations as grim-faced and intolerantly righteous as their buildings. What is most striking, and has left the most pervasive evidence in the hundreds of chapels dotted all over the south west landscape and townscape, are the intensely local character and loyalties of chapel life in general and Methodism in particular. New meetings and regroupings were continually springing up in response to local needs and circumstances, their fluidity and

vitality allowing them to respond quickly to the ever-changing society of the mining landscapes.

In 1851 a unique national census of churches and chapels gave a striking indication of the strength of Nonconformity in Devon. Of 1,297 places of

Above
Former chapel, Merrivale Quarry, Dartmoor

Right
Former chapel, Taw Green, near South Tawton

TAW GREEN
BAPTIST CHAPEL
1903

worship, no less than 748 were non-Anglican with 379 Methodist, 142 Congre-
gationalist, 112 Baptist, 12 Unitarian and 8 Quaker. Although Methodism is the
largest denomination in the south west, it is a late coalition of fiercely independent congregations, of which the largest single grouping was the Bible
Christians. They were founded in 1815 at Lake Farm, Shebbear in the remote
border country between Devon and Cornwall by William O'Bryan, who had
defected from the Wesleyan Methodists to pursue his own evangelical work;
from this small beginning at its height the movement claimed 175 chapels.

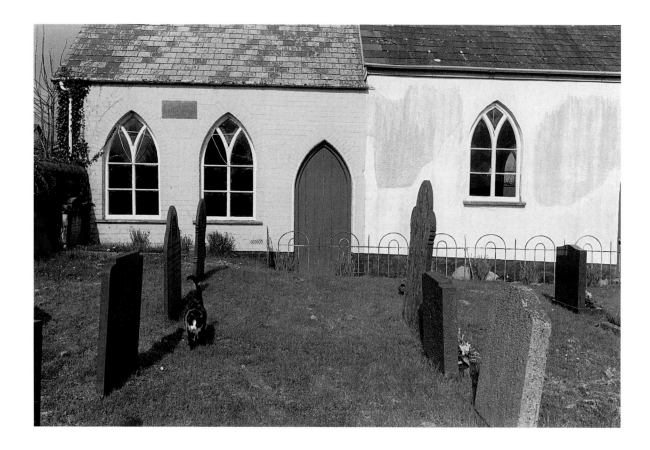

Local trusteeship ensured that all decisions about building matters were locally
determined, so it was more likely to be the local builder who was employed to
design and build a chapel rather than an architect from a far-away town. It was
this that produced the engaging pluriformity that makes it impossible to categorise chapels into neat architectural sequences. Somehow the resultant
kaleidoscope of styles and building materials faithfully reflects the aspirations
as well as the inspiration of the chapel builders.

The chapel arguably exercised more cultural influence than Anglicanism in most of Cornwall and much of Devon for most of the nineteenth and twentieth centuries. Urban Nonconformity still flourishes, but rural chapels have faced a dramatic decline with hundreds already made redundant and sold for 'conversion', and many more certain to join them. Nonconformists are sometimes criticised for the ease with which they dispose of their unwanted buildings, apparently careless of their own history as well as their significance to the wider community. But perhaps their lightness of hold on these built expressions of faith has something commendable that other denominations prone to building obsession could learn from. If, as is claimed, their purpose is to point to the beyond in our midst, then it is right that they are ultimately to be seen as transient, no more than tabernacles in the wilderness.

Left

Former Baptist chapel and Sunday school, Kingscott, St Giles in the Wood

Above
All Saints church, Dunterton

Churchyard

There is the mellifluous perfection of those Somerset towers, sailing high over the Levels and soaring above the Mendips; and there is the rich embellishment of the west country's town churches like Totnes and Launceston, rivalling even their castles for pre-eminence in their townscapes. But the ecclesiastical vernacular of the far south west is the small church that suddenly appears on the horizon of the deepest countryside, enfolded in lanes, fields and woods: so modest in its stature that its pinnacles are curiously oversized as if to give it an extra lift skyward. In hamlet after hamlet, occasionally next to the squire's house like Bradstone, Kelly and Tetcott, sometimes in a farmyard as at Luffincott and Warkleigh, or even alone in the fields like All Saints at Dunterton, these little churches are the most tangible expression of a parish so spread out over the landscape that it is otherwise only discernible as a name on the map.

Before finally reaching the church, the visitor first has to pass through the churchyard. The churchyard can be a place to linger, as often happens naturally at a wedding – and may even be perfect for a quiet doze on a summer afternoon – but it is unlikely to be mentioned in the guidebook: it is simply taken for granted as the space passed over on the way to see the church. If it happens at all, the exploration of the churchyard will be limited to a duty round of the church exterior and to a nod at one or two headstones with amusing rustic verses which the guide book might mention. Perhaps it is simply that there are many good excuses, besides an all-consuming passion for church architecture, to cover up the awkward truth that here, surrounded by the mortal remains of our predecessors, we come face to face with the certainty of our own mortality.

Yet, looked at in the perspective of history, churchyards deal in continuity as much as finality. This is true in the most obvious sense that headstones usually represent only the latest layer of humanity laid to rest there. They date from the eighteenth and nineteenth centuries when an emerging prosperous middle class began to imitate the long-standing predilection of their superiors to honour their dead with funerary monuments, often producing exquisite works of art and cluttering up the best bits of the church interior at one and the same time. Inscribed headstones became a real art form (it is often possible to trace local craftsmen's names on the base of the stone) but these marked

graves had to use ground previously buried over for many centuries. These medieval burials often follow even earlier occupation and veneration of the site before it was taken over by Christianity, reinforcing the sense that this plot of earth has a spiritual power that has always been inclusive.

For death has a way of ironing out some of life's more meaningless distinctions. Although children for baptism or couples for marriage are less familiar visitors to church today, funerals can still command the presence of the

Left
Churchyard, Charles

Above
Looking at the polaroid after the wedding

wider community. Subsoil from a newly dug grave, fresh flowers over a recent burial, small posies or large bunches on the more remembered graves, a cluster of tablets or plaques marking the interment of ashes: all are guarantors of the abiding specialness of the churchyard for the community beyond the boundaries of church membership. Unless the historic churchyard is vast in proportion to the size of the present-day settlement, like the great tree-lined enclosure at Chawleigh, this will find expression in a modern extension of the churchyard adjacent, or as near as possible, to the original. If sometimes of necessity it is a little distance away, no matter; the present burial ground at Chulmleigh is over the road from the church but still seems overseen by its presence.

The entrance will usually be through a simple wooden or wrought iron gate, sometimes dignified by stone or brick piers and a modest ironwork overthrow to hold a lantern. Older lychgates tend to be relatively functional affairs to shelter the bearers and coffin before the final journey but there are some spectacularly aggrandised examples from the late nineteenth century onwards: the splendid Arts and Crafts specimen at Warkleigh looks surprised to find itself in the middle of a farmyard. However entered, there are no hard edges to the boundaries of the rural churchyard. There may be a retaining wall in local stone if the church and churchyard occupy a relatively elevated site in the settlement, as at Cadeleigh in Devon or Egloskerry in Cornwall, making the churchyard more visible and open to its community. Elsewhere the boundaries will be formed by hedges and trees on earth banks, just like the surrounding fields.

This sense of immemorial belonging to the landscape is confirmed by the traditional management of churchyards as hay meadows, often reservoirs of flora and fauna lost outside, where the grass is cut only once or twice a year; or as pasture with seasonal sheep grazing for a closer cut. Headstones seem at home in grass and wild flowers especially when strewn with snowdrops and narcissi in spring and at the early summer peak before the first cut. Left to their own devices older headstones come to rest at various improbable angles, cocking a snook at the last enemy but also nicely mirroring life's relationships which are not always at the true vertical or right angle intended: some headstones even look like families or groups of friends talking to each other. They look miser-

Above
Waiting for the bride, St Mary Magdalene, Chulmleigh

Overleaf
Churchyard, St Giles in the Wood

In memory of DANIEL
TANTON by Firing off
a Gun it Burft the Breech
of which sunk in his Head
where it remained 9 weeks
on extraction of which he
expired V20 of ... 179...

able when forced to stand to attention in ordered ranks around the edge of the churchyard. Left alone they testify to the diversity of the human spirit, at their best in streaming wet when the colours of local slates come alive. Some inscriptions are amusing, some unbearable in their maudlin sentiment, but most bear direct witness to bereavement's sense of devastating, inconsolable loss.

These very personal histories writ large across rural churchyards become social history told as it really was: the briefness of life's span before the twentieth century; the frequency of infant mortality; the social distinctions that were carried beyond the grave, like the practice of burying the poor on the sunless northern side. In the twentieth century it is the war memorials that often stir the emotions, vividly recording the irruption of the wider world's politics into these isolated and fiercely independent communities: sometimes the list of names seems implausibly long in parishes where not a single house is visible from the churchyard. So churchyards come to represent some of the deepest roots that individuals, families and communities can put down: and the place becomes truly unique, evoking a sense of belonging unlike anywhere else on earth.

Beyond the churchyard, life goes on. At St Enodoc in Cornwall, John Betjeman's simple but elegantly engraved gravestone in Delabole slate seems perfectly at home surrounded by tamarisks and sand dunes as golf balls whiz past on the neighbouring links and the cries of children playing on Daymer Bay waft into the churchyard. And in deeper country the churchyard is similarly absorbed into the local scene: sheep and cattle grazing in the next field; farm machinery peering over the hedge; the sounds and smells of farm life filling the air. At Highhampton the churchyard commands a view over the fields and farms of lowland Devon towards Dartmoor rising to its most impressive northern heights on the horizon. Once in a lifetime it is worth being in such a place at sunrise, to know the heart of the place in the company of the local saints who lie all around, facing east, waiting for a new day to begin.

Left
Early morning, Highampton churchyard

Above
Bell ropes, St James, Iddesleigh

Belfry

A serious house on serious earth it is,
In whose blent air all our compulsions meet,
Are recognised, and robed as destinies.

Philip Larkin, *Church Going*

The religious ambiguities that characterise England find perfect expression in Philip Larkin's poem, reflecting the continuing power of a church to draw people inside its doors and to inspire contemplation about its meaning despite dwindling church membership. Such paradoxes apply with special force to the belfry, hidden high away and inaccessible most of the time, yet the source of a sound so stupendous that it can command attention even in a noisy world. Bell-ringing remains a mysterious society, whose activities are nevertheless capable of vibrating medieval walls, carrying the music of the bells for miles beyond the walls of the churchyard and, in the plangent melancholy of a half-muffled peal echoing around a town or rolling across open fields, bringing you to your knees.

Towards the end of a gentle exploration of a small Devon church like Iddesleigh, after the spaces, silences and smells have been savoured, perhaps only on the way out, the eye may be drawn to the west end and, against the light of the west window, there may be a glimpse of bell ropes drawn high up out of reach of mischief. In many small west country churches the bells are rung from the ground floor of the tower that is not only ringing chamber but vestry, broom cupboard and head-quarters of the flower arrangers. Here the ropes hang above the delightful clutter of worship, sometimes not even a curtain to hide service books, registers, flower vases, candles, the remnants of the Christmas crib or the Easter sepulchre, together with the odd bottle of 'Vino Sacro', the commercial brand of communion wine.

In larger churches there will be a modest door which, although always locked, promises access to the tower. Opened by an ancient key, this narrow door leads to steeply-winding stone steps. Climbing them arouses a strange excitement, even a hint of danger, as the nostrils fill with the air of somewhere different, slight dampness mingled with rope and matting. Eventually another small door gives entry into the ringing chamber itself. It is simple and work-manlike, hung with fading certificates of past achievements in ringing competitions and heroic peals, perhaps a notice about the maker of the bell-ropes and a stern warning about the state of readiness of the bells above. Even when empty of ringers, it is the ropes that enthrall, their looming presence filling the space, their woollen sallies – the hand hold for the ringer – lighting up the chamber with bright splashes of colour and the end of the ropes disappearing upwards through small holes in the ceiling into the bell chamber above.

Another steep climb finally gives access to the bell chamber itself, where the sheer awesomeness of the bell-ringing enterprise can begin to be appreciated. Here in the high tower, exposed to wind and weather through open louvres of slate, stone or timber that let out the sound of the bells to the world, the full majesty of the bells is now revealed. Prodigious in scale and ancient in years, they are formidable evidence of the bell-founders' craft over the centuries, sometimes even of medieval casting, and often hung in bell-frames that may also be centuries old. It is humbling to think of these huge pieces of metal being cast, hauled up the tower and hung so long ago, and then used more or less continuously ever since. And when the realisation dawns that to make these bells 'speak', as ringers have it, they are not just chimed but have to be raised by pulling the rope around the large wheel attached to each bell, so that at each stroke they will swing through nearly a full circle, then the extraordinary skill employed in ringing can be admired.

Though the ringing chamber is a close society with its own traditions and rituals, its membership includes all ages and backgrounds, and its hospitality to visitors is generous. Ringing demands good teamwork, the ringers standing

Left
Bell ringers, St Lawrence, Sheepwash

in a loose circle facing each other, the tail end of the rope in one hand, the sally between both. Then at the order of the tower captain the ringer of the lightest bell – the treble – will pull down on the sally, striking the clapper to the bell, the others following quickly, watching and listening intently as the bells begin to rise, furiously fast at first but gradually easing and lengthening out as the bells near the top of their wheels. As the rhythm of the bells is found, the quiet intensity of the ringing chamber contrasts with the towering sound echoing around

outside. At such times the ringing chamber works like a beautifully oiled machine. The flashes of colour as the sallies rise and plummet, the calls of the tower captain, the very physical yet disciplined movement of the ringers, all mark the intimate partnership between the team and the bells in their charge.

The ringing world has strong regional traditions. The west country is a stronghold of call-change ringing in which each bell is called individually by the tower captain into a different place in the striking sequence. It is quite different from method ringing – sometimes called 'scientific' in the west country –

Left
Rehanging the bells, St James, Chawleigh

Above
Harvest Festival decorations, St James, Iddesleigh

Overleaf
St James church tower from Westpark, Iddesleigh

where the bells are rung to predetermined mathematically ordered sequences in which each bell is changing places at every stroke. The names of the methods are evocative in themselves – Grandsire, Stedman or Kent Treble Bob Major – and method ringing is accompanied by apparently random calls of 'Bob' and 'Single' from the tower captain. What matters to all ringers is that the bell in their charge is so handled that it contributes with exactly right striking to the incomparable, immemorial sound of rounded, rolling rhythm that sings out of the belfry into the air of England.

Deans of ancient cathedral cities and churchwardens of remote country churches receive frequent and often vehement complaints about the ringing of church bells, and even the striking of the church clock. The sound of a tradition that can be traced back in unbroken continuity to the medieval world deserves to be heard with respect. For centuries church bells have been employed at times of national importance to proclaim messages of triumph or disaster, exultation or grief. And in quieter times, week by week faithful ringers have made them speak of continuity and belonging in the local community. Many medieval bells had simple prayers engraved on them, making it possible to hear their sound as the pouring out of timeless blessings on all around – or, as Larkin might have it, mediating in wordless language between that serious house in which they are set and the serious earth over which their message flows.

Left
Exeter Cathedral, south tower

Above
Storm, New Year's Day, Westward Ho!

Weather

To the summer visitor who happens on a spell of fair settled weather there are many beaches in the west country that live up to those pictures in tourist brochures which portray the peninsula as an English, or Cornish, version of 'The Riviera' and even, in the shelter of Tresco Abbey's gardens on the Isles of Scilly, a sub-tropical paradise. Such images have long been used to promote the distinctive character of the region, perhaps most famously in those atmospheric photographs and posters that used to decorate the passenger compartments and waiting rooms of the Great Western Railway. Its favourable climate has attracted visitors ever since the wealthy were first wooed to its southern coastal resorts for the sake of their health in the early nineteenth century. It is different here: this most far-flung limb of southern England juts out into the Atlantic, is warmed by the Gulf Stream and passed over by prevailing moisture-laden winds, and so enjoys a climate that, in the favourite words of the guide books, is reckoned to be 'moist', 'mild', 'soft' and 'equable'.

But just as its beaches do not constitute the south west landscape so its climate is not its weather. The difference is crucial. Few guide books talk about weather, presumably because climate is, as it were, the theory, weather the practice. Weather is what we actually experience, what we go out in every day, a subject of such importance in our lives that it even influences what we wear, the one certain topic of conversation with complete strangers, the talisman of a successful or disastrous holiday. At a time when the task of sustaining local distinctiveness seems like an unequal struggle against the odds, local weather really ought to be celebrated - and tourist boards ought to tell it like it is. After all, in today's high-tech world of outdoor pursuits surely there can be no such thing as bad weather, merely inappropriate clothing.

So to stand awe-struck before the force of a winter gale crashing huge cold waves against the cliffs is as memorable as summer's clear turquoise sea quietly lapping over white sand at the same spot six months earlier. Those October days when the vivid purple and russet colours of the moors can be viewed in such clear air that the prospect seems to be of half of England are all the more miraculous a few weeks later in the bitter cold of a moorland drizzle when you cannot see your hand in front of your face. The strange otherness of that great spread of country north of Dartmoor, so amiable when lost in a sleepy sun-drenched haze, is only really explained when winter brings rain sweeping in day after day to turn those blissful lanes, fields, and farmyards into a landscape of intractable, unyielding, unforgiving mud.

Those who have lived their lives in the west know why the moors are sparsely populated; why settlements along an essentially hostile coastline are crammed into the rare safe havens; why trees and hedges anywhere exposed to the wind are bent double; why farms were not built with picture windows to enjoy the view but were carefully sited for shelter and the best management of their land; why the exposed faces of cob are eroded and pitted into weather-beaten profiles. The realisation dawns that we are not the masters of creation

Left
Cows at Balls Farm, Merton

Above
George Ayre and his flock, Ashwell, Dolton

Overleaf
Storm at Ramscliffe, Beaford

we are sometimes tempted to believe we have become. It is left to the weather to put us in our place; for a light snowfall to bring the mighty automobile to an impotent standstill not just on the moors; for fog or high seas to cut off Lundy and the Scillies for days on end; for floods to turn the Somerset Levels and other wide estuaries into inland seas.

And it is at best a half-truth to describe the south west as 'soft' and 'moist'. It is true that two long irregular coastlines combine with many estuaries to carry

the sea's influence far inland, magically expressed in those secret gardens stuffed with camellias, rhododendrons, tree ferns and even the occasional palm that are hidden away in sheltered crevices in the south coast of Devon and Cornwall. But the upstanding fastnesses of old rocks that are found down the length of the peninsula, starting in the east with the Quantocks and Exmoor, peaking in Dartmoor and Bodmin Moor, and still strong in Penwith, profoundly affect rainfall, temperature, cloud cover and wind exposure. 'Harsh' and 'cold' would be better epithets for these moors: not for nothing were they described

Left
Ivor Brock feeding sheep in a blizzard, Millhams, Dolton

Above
Snowy track, Riddlecombe

as 'mountains' by travellers in previous centuries before our age of global travel, allied to the security of car-bound exploration, reduced our respect for them. It should not be so. It is still possible to be awed by their towering presence, no more so than when looking towards Dartmoor from the north west on a winter's afternoon when Larkin's 'high-builded clouds' heighten their dramatic silhouette and their peaks are highlighted in snow.

What seems to have permeated the consciousness of most travellers to Devon over the centuries is the wetness of the county, though rainfall is very unevenly distributed so that Princetown on western Dartmoor has well over 80 inches a year while Exeter has less than 30. Rain drove at least one Abbot of Tavistock Abbey to drink: H P R Finberg records of the unfortunate fourteenth-century Abbot Bonus that 'a native of sun-soaked Gascony found himself living on the edge of Dartmoor under grey skies and what must have seemed to him like incessant rain. To keep the damp out he called for wine, and small wonder if his potations grew at times excessive'. Four centuries later Keats was famously prevented by the Devon rain from viewing the scenery for five successive days: when he finally emerged it was with the waspish comment that 'the green is beautiful, as they say, and pity it is that it is amphibious'. It took until the second half of the twentieth century for the raw, hard, muddy reality of the west country farm to be powerfully evoked in the poetry of Ted Hughes.

There is indeed a special sense of being open to the weather in the west. It is partly the inevitable consequence of living on a peninsula, the feeling that the land is running out as we go westward, all the time diminishing against the great encompassing Atlantic and the ever-widening sky. Long coastlines to north and south, the drowned river valleys and a scatter of islands afford generous opportunities for the merging of sea and sky and reflection on the vastness of it all. But not just there. The openness of the uplands and moors, their lack of tree cover and settlements, helps lift up our eyes to the hills to savour the air and watch the remodelling of clouds like the endless reworking of a Constable or Turner sky. And after sunset, the darkness of the west's night sky, mostly still free from light pollution, promises different riches in the endless constellations of other worlds starring the blackness.

Ephemeral, ever changing: if that is true of weather, then how much more so of its most intangible elements, air and light. The clarity of the air is nowhere more wonderfully expressed than deep in woods on lichen-covered branches especially luminous when trees are bare of leaves and caught in winter sunlight. And it is the quality of light that perhaps best conveys the elusive distinctiveness of the west and which has for long drawn artists here. Over the last century this has become so celebrated that in the far west of the Penwith peninsula Newlyn and St. Ives evolved their own schools of painting alongside pottery and other arts. If there is ever any doubt about the way something as indefinable as light can influence our view of the world, it is worth going to stand inside the canopy of the new Tate at St. Ives, to feel this great building mediating between the still luminosity of Porthmeor beach and the light caught in the treasures of its galleries inside and, whatever the weather, to know its power.

Above
Peter Beacham writing notes, Church Stile, Monkokehampton

Further Reading

Beacham, Peter, (ed.). *Devon Building: An Introduction to Local Traditions*, Devon Books, 1990, second edition, 1995.

Betjeman, John. *Cornwall* and *Devon* in the *Shell Guides*, Faber & Faber, 1934 and 1935, revised 1964, and 1955 [by Brian Watson] and 1975 [by Ann Jellicoe and Roger Mayne] respectively.

Cherry, Bridget and Niklaus Pevsner. *Devon*, Penguin Books, 1990, reprinted 1992.

Cornwell, John. *Earth to Earth*, Allen Lane, 1982.

Fleming, Andrew. *The Dartmoor Reaves*, Batsford, 1988.

Hamilton, Peter. *An English Eye: The Photographs of James Ravilious*, Devon Books, 1998.

Higham, Robert, (ed.). *Landscape and Townscape in the South West*, University of Exeter Press, 1989.

Hoskins, W G. *Devon*, Collins, 1954; Commemorative Edition with introduction by Peter Beacham, Devon Books, 1992.

Hoskins, W G. *The Making of the English Landscape*, Hodder and Stoughton, 1955, new edition revised by Christopher Taylor, 1988.

Hughes, Ted. *The Hawk in the Rain*, 1957; *Season Songs*, 1976; *Moortown*, 1979, all may be found reprinted in *Selected Poems, 1957–1981*, Faber & Faber, 1981.

Marshall, William. *Rural Economy of the West of England*, 1796.

Orchards – A Guide to Local Conservation, [with photographs by James Ravilious], Common Ground, 1989.

Orme, Nicholas. *Unity and Variety – A History of the Church in Devon and Cornwall,* University of Exeter Press, 1991.

Rackham, Oliver. *The History of the Countryside,* J. M. Dent, 1986.

Rackham, Oliver. *Trees and Woodland in the British Landscape,* J. M. Dent, 1976, revised edition 1990.

Ravilious, James and Robin. *The Heart of the Country,* Scolar Press, 1980.

Ravilious, James. *A Corner of England,* Devon Books in association with the Lutterworth Press, 1995, reprinted 1996 and 1999.

Thorne, Roger. *The Last Bible Christians – Their Church in Devon in 1907.* Trans. Devon Assoc. Vol. 107, 1975, 47–75.

Todd, Malcolm. *The South West to AD1000,* Longman, 1987.

Vancouver, Charles. *General View of the Agriculture of the County of Devon,* 1808, reprinted by David and Charles, 1969.

Index of Tailpieces

Page 15
George Ayre's boots, Dolton

Page 25
Bullocks near Kingscott

Page 35
Hat stand, Exmoor farm

Page 45
Abandoned plough, Mousehole, Iddesleigh

Page 55
Cider press, Higher Hacknell, Burrington

Page 65
Flower show entries, Dolton

Page 75
Ruined cob cottage, Broadwoodkelly

Page 85
Cow shed, Cuppers Piece, Beaford

Page 95
Old machinery, Newbridge quarry, Dolton

Page 107
Church parade, Hatherleigh

Page 117
Gravestones, Highampton

Page 127
Beneath the tower, St David, Thelbridge

Page 137
Closing the gate, Ashreigney

Page 140
Greenhouse, North Walk, Chulmleigh

Map

Places in north Devon photographed by James Ravilious for this book

EXMOOR

BARNSTAPLE

Swimbridge ●

● Charles

A39

Westward
Ho! ●

BIDEFORD

River Taw

A377

South Molton ●

A361

Chittlehampton

To Bampton

River Mole

A373

Atherington ●

● Chittlehamholt

Torrington

● St. Giles
in the Wood   ● Ebberly

Kingscott ●

Roborough ●

Burrington ●

● Kings Nympton

A388

A386

● Beaford
Riddlecombe ●

Bridge Reeve ●
Ashreigney ●

● Chulmleigh
● Chawleigh

To Tiverton

Merton ●

● Dolton

● Hollocombe

Thelbridge ●

● Dowland

Lapford ●

● Iddesleigh

● Winkleigh

Coldridge ●

Sheepwash ●

River Okement

River Taw

Down St Mary ●

A377

River Torridge

Broadwoodkelly ●

● Highampton
A3072

● Hatherleigh

A386

A3072

To Crediton

To Holsworthy

River Yeo

● Northlew
● Ashbury

● Beaworthy

● Taw
Green

North

Major roads

OKEHAMPTON

To Exeter

0   Miles   5

South
Zeal

A30

0   Kilometres   5

● Meldon   DARTMOOR

CARTOGRAPHICS by: John Hunt, FBCart.S

Going home,
Frank Pickard and Flash, Dolton

James Ravilious (1939–1999)
died before printing of this book could be completed